NEW WAYS FOR LIFE™

Instructor's Guide

Life Skills for Young People

AUTHORS:
Susie Rayner, Mediator
Bill Eddy, LCSW, Esq.

A project of High Conflict Institute

A Note to the Reader

This publication is designed to provide accurate and authoritative information about the subject matters covered. It is sold with the understanding that neither the authors nor publisher are rendering legal, mental health, medical or other professional services, either directly or indirectly. If expert assistance, legal services or counseling is needed, the services of a competent professional should be sought. Names and identifying information of private individuals have been changed to preserve anonymity. Neither the authors nor the publisher shall be liable or responsible for any loss or damage allegedly arising as a consequence of your use or application of any information or suggestions in this book.

ISBN-13: 978-1950057085

Publisher
Unhooked Books, an imprint of High Conflict Institute Press
7701 E. Indian School Rd., Ste. F
Scottsdale, AZ 85251 USA

Contents

FOR COACHES / TEACHERS / MENTORS / PARENTS

Letter From Us to You v

About this *Instructor's Guide* vii

Chapter One: The 4 Big Skills for Life 1

Chapter Two: Teaching an Individual Young Person. 7

Chapter Three: Teaching *New Ways for Life*™ as a Class . . . 21

Sessions Overview 23

    Session 1: Managing Emotions 26

    Session 2: Flexible Thinking. 51

    Session 3: Moderate Behavior and BIFF Responses 64

    Session 4: Checking Yourself 82

Feelings Word Guide 92

Certificate of Completion 93

About the Authors 94

Letter From Us to You

New Ways for Life™ is a program that is specifically designed for young people ages 12 to 17 years old. We are excited that you are interested in using this new way of teaching skills that they can use throughout their lives. We consider this a collaboration between us, you and the young people you will be working with. With that in mind, there are several things we would like you to think about.

This is a simple, structured method based on the four big skills of the *New Ways for Families*® method for adults and children developed by High Conflict Institute over the past ten years. While these skills may seem rather simple, it is through the repetition of these skills that people really learn them and gain confidence that they can remember to apply them in the future. Don't be afraid to just keep repeating them and keep it simple.

Feel free to share these skills with anyone. The more people who understand and use these four big skills, the easier it is for everyone to remember them. We appreciate that you may have had experience with teaching other methods and skills. But we want you to keep the focus on these four big skills without introducing a lot of other concepts that may be brilliant, but a distraction from the repetition of these four skills.

These skills can be used in a wide variety of situations, from easy to extremely hostile or dangerous. We understand that the teens you are working with may be facing extreme circumstances (family violence, school bullying, suicidal thoughts, coronavirus impact and so forth), or very positive protected lives at this time. Since we leave space for exercises using the young person's own situations, you can give suggestions that fit their own lives. The same skills apply to all of these settings, but the way they are implemented may vary. Don't let them tell you that this method is too simplistic for them. Keeping it simple is what makes it powerful.

Whether you are instructing them on a one-to-one basis (such as a coach, parent, mentor, or counselor) or whether you are going to be teaching them in a group setting (teacher, youth leader, facilitator, or other role), we encourage you to take a friendly approach that indicates a sense of being in this together, such as being on the "same level." After all, we could all be better at using these skills.

Avoid talking down to your young people. We strongly feel that the key to creating change doesn't just lie in the actual teaching or coaching alone, but in the relationship that is established with your young people. Sometimes they feel controlled or unimportant, or that what they think doesn't matter. When a young person feels like this, they are less likely to learn and will have little motivation to make changes and establish relationships with a perceived authority figure.

New Ways for Life™ is about helping young people learn that they can control their reactions to situations – they have the power within themselves to control their emotions, behavior and thinking. No one is telling them what to do. Everyone is on the same level! We want them to feel comfortable, empowered, and heard.

We hope you enjoy working with youth to create everlasting change. It is our mission to provide these skills to as many young people as possible—in whatever circumstance—so that they can deal with the stresses of life in a managed, flexible and safe way.

Yours in life,
Susie Rayner and Bill Eddy

About this *Instructor's Guide*

Susie Rayner gets the credit for writing most of this *Instructor's Guide* and developing materials that can go with it. She adapted it from the **4 Big Skills** of *New Ways for Families®*, a short-term counseling and coaching method developed by Bill Eddy in several Workbooks and Manuals over the past ten years. *New Ways for Families®* is designed to help parents strengthen conflict-resolution and co-parenting skills before big decisions are made about their transitioning families before, during and after separation or divorce. It is designed to save courts time, to save parents money, and to protect children as their families re-organize in new ways.

What we have done with the *New Ways for Life™* program is taken some key points, adapted them for a different audience (young people) and packaged it all together to give them some incredibly valuable tools for everyday life.

It is designed for use by any instructor working on these skills with a young person either individually (such as a coach, parent, mentor, or counselor) or in a group (teacher, youth leader, facilitator, or other role). This Guide parallels the Youth Journal, which has a moderate amount of instruction and many writing exercises.

We realize that the young people learning these skills will come from a wide range of situations. Some may be very young 12-year-olds and others may be very mature 17-year-olds. Some may be homeless or dealing with drug addiction or family violence. Some may be struggling to make it to school or not. Some may be well-to-do and have a lot of resources and self-confidence. It will be up to you to help the young person in front of you to apply these skills to their own life situation, especially in discussions and in the writing exercises.

Additional materials: When it comes to teaching these skills as a class, the Guide refers to using PowerPoint slides, games and other materials. Those do not come with this *Instructor's Guide*. Instead, they are available at a nominal fee from the website: www.NewWays4Life. com. You do not need to have those materials for a young person to use and benefit from the Youth Journal. However, those materials can greatly enhance teaching this method as a class.

You are encouraged to get a copy of the Youth Journal for yourself as you prepare to work with your young person. That way you can see the questions they are asked for their writing exercises and think of situations you could discuss that might relate personally to them. Feel free to suggest additional writing exercises, so long as they reinforce the **4 Big Skills** for life.

Let's get started.

CHAPTER ONE

The 4 Big Skills for Life
By Bill Eddy

I developed the *New Ways for Families*® method after working with children, youth and parents involved in high conflict separations and divorces. I saw the same patterns of problems occurring over and over again. Rather than focusing on what family members were doing poorly or wrong, I wanted to teach them patterns of new behavior that could help them do things well in the future. The focus has always been on the future, not the past; on skills not problems; on keeping it simple and easy to remember, rather than too complicated.

I took everything I learned from my prior careers as a teacher, counselor, lawyer and mediator and put it into a simple method—*New Ways*™ for doing things better. I began to use this skills-training approach in my mediations, which became *New Ways for Mediation*®. I was asked to help employees and managers who were in trouble in the workplace and co-developed *New Ways for Work*™. There were four main areas where some people seemed to repeatedly get stuck:

1. They had rigid, all-or-nothing thinking.

2. They couldn't manage their own emotions.

3. They sometimes or often used extreme behavior.

4. They were preoccupied with blaming others and didn't take responsibility themselves.

Most teachers, counselors, parents and others tend to tell people who are stuck in these ways to just stop what they're doing. Just stop! But that doesn't give them something to do instead—a replacement behavior. Just as alcoholics can't "just say no," Alcoholics Anonymous teaches new replacement behaviors instead. It works.

Many teachers, counselors, parents and others tend to also focus just on the "bad behavior," without understanding the thinking and feelings that lead up to that difficult behavior. Young people often don't know why they did what they did, so they just become defensive.

I realized that telling them what NOT TO DO usually just got into an argument. This was often true with teenagers. So, I wanted to focus on WHAT TO DO instead. In every setting I was working in, it became clear that the focus needed to be on finding new ways of teaching these four big skills:

The 4 Big Skills

1. Flexible Thinking
2. Managed Emotions
3. Moderate Behavior
4. Checking Themselves

Within each of these **4 Big Skills**, there are several little skills. This is how the *Youth Journal* is designed. For example, with managed emotions, we teach young people how to give themselves encouraging statements as well as how to find someone "neutral" to talk to, and how to take a break. They learn the little skills and the big concept as well, which is managing their emotions. Rather than tell them what they "should" do, we tell them "how" they can do it.

We also talk about how flexible thinking will help them manage their emotions, how managed emotions will help them have moderate behavior, and how checking themselves will keep them on track. These skills are all interconnected. It also helps to explain ways in which these skills will help them succeed in life, in close relationships, at work and in their larger communities. These are leadership skills and conflict resolution skills. You can remind them of these benefits as you teach this method.

Goals

You can also ask them what their own goals are under each of these **4 Big Skills**. Perhaps they want to manage their emotions better when a good friend occasionally criticizes them. Perhaps they want to use flexible thinking when applying for a volunteer opportunity or a job in a new area of interest. Perhaps they want to use moderate behavior when told they can't go to a party.

When you connect what you are teaching to a person's own goals, it opens their mind and motivates more behavior change than just telling them it's good for them. Sometimes even picturing themselves doing the behavior that they want can be motivating.

Benefits

Learning the **4 Big Skills** has a lot of benefits for young people. In addition to helping them succeed in the future as adults, these skills will also help them right away in making friends, solving routine problems, and confronting big challenges with confidence and creative thinking. In many ways, the *New Ways for Life™* skills are self-management skills. By managing themselves better, it will become easier to make friends and to keep friendships. By managing themselves better, it will help them succeed in school and unknown new situations.

Social Pressures

These **4 Big Skills** are more important than ever for young people to learn because the larger cultural environment is teaching negative lessons (the opposite of what we teach) these days with high conflict thinking, feeling and behaving. These are demonstrated constantly on television, in the movies, and in the news. World leaders and celebrities are modeling the negative lessons that we don't want young people to learn. Yet, these cultural leaders are often looked up to by many young people and many adults.

You may have to explain how these negative lessons undermine people in the long run. Sadly, it is getting harder for young people to know what is normal or good behavior. You and this Youth Journal may be very significant in their life development. It would be beneficial to discuss with your young person finding someone who they can share these positive lessons with for support and encouragement of their own learning. You can also explain how the *New Ways*™ skills will help them cope with negative people in their lives, whether adults or peers.

Stressful Circumstances

Today's young people are feeling more stress from the long-term impact of the coronavirus and the economic downturn, and the effect of these on their own schooling, their parents' jobs, general health, fewer opportunities and possible lack of support from those they are close to. It can help to talk directly about these frustrations and how to apply the **4 Big Skills** to dealing with them. Giving themselves encouraging statements may be hard, but even more important these days. Times change and life is a series of ups and downs, which is why we have the human ability to adapt and grow under any circumstance.

Some youth are facing family separation, family violence (their own or a parent), addiction, bullying at school or at work, and sometimes even suicidal thoughts or self-injury. It's important to help them get to a professional who can assist with these problems. A coach, teacher or mentor should not attempt to counsel the youth or guess at what they need. Get them to someone familiar with these types of problems.

Mental Health Issues

Approximately 25% of adolescents 12 to 17 years old have a diagnosable mental health issue these days. Most of these are untreated, and the young person may feel alone with their problems or try to hide them. If you become aware of such problems, try to help them in getting to a professional who can assist them most effectively.

However, practicing the **4 Big Skills** should fit into any reasonable mental health assistance they receive. You can ask how you can support professionals who may work with your young person. Most mental health problems are helped by the person learning and practicing these same **4 Big Skills** as a part of their treatment or recovery. But it can't be the whole treatment. Get a professional involved who is trained in working with adolescents.

You Are Very Important

With everything I have said above, please realize how important you can be to a young person's development and growth. Even just one caring adult can make a difference in a young person's life. The transition from child to adult is fraught with challenges but learning skills for dealing with life's adversities from understanding adults is a big part of what the teenage years are all about. How you demonstrate these **4 Big Skills** in your own interactions with your young person will matter the most.

The rest of this book explains the "how" of teaching *New Ways for Life™*. The next chapter focuses on teaching an individual young person. The following chapters focus on teaching a group of young people in a class format.

CHAPTER TWO

Teaching an Individual Young Person
By Bill Eddy

You may be a professional counselor, a parent, a coach or a mentor for someone who is taking this course in life skills. It's very important to keep your role clear, so that you do not try to become his or her counselor unless that is the relationship that you already have. The focus of *New Ways for Life™* is learning skills, not getting deep into psychological issues or becoming responsible for the young person's life problems. Neither of these will help if you are in the role of instructor with this method. It is a teaching role only. Make that clear to the youth you are working with. You can talk about issues, but in the context teaching these skills and applying them to the teenager's situation.

Working with the *Youth Journal*

The Youth Journal is divided into the **4 Big Skills** as four chapters simply titled:

Skill 1.   Managing Your Emotions

Skill 2.   Flexible Thinking

Skill 3.   Moderate Behavior

Skill 4.   Checking Yourself

Each Skill chapter has explanations and writing exercises. Plan to meet four times for one hour each to assist the teen by discussing the lessons contained with each skill, by answering any questions they may have, and reviewing what they have written and discussing it with them. Plan your hour so that you both can stay focused and feel that you accomplished something each time. However, there is time for relaxed conversation related to the skill you are on. You can talk about how to apply it in many different settings.

It is okay if the young person has not read the lesson or written the exercises before your meeting. He or she can discuss it and write the exercises while with you. It's a no blame, no shame approach, so no need to make working in the Journal a conflict. But encourage the teen to read it beforehand and write the exercises in the Journal or on a separate paper to discuss with you before they put it in the Journal.

This is their Journal to do with as they want. It's expected that your young person will want to keep it for future reference, but that is up to them.

Sharing Your Experiences

When working with adolescents, it really helps to share some of your own personal examples, so long as they don't become the focus of the discussion. You could say, "Would you like to know about a situation like this that I had once?" If the teen says, "Yes," then you can go ahead. If not, then drop it. This is an example of giving choices which is part of "Flexible Thinking" (Skill 2 in their Journal).

Only share appropriate experiences that help in understanding the lesson and are not too personal. For example, don't go into the history of your divorce, first sexual experience or anything else that can become too emotionally intense for them or for you. You want these lessons to be positive to show how you learned or used one of these skills, not to show how badly something went (unless it has a good ending with a good lesson).

Emotional Boundaries

Young people can get overwhelmed if they feel responsible for someone else's feelings or situation and don't have the emotional boundaries yet to protect themselves. But emotional boundaries are a part of "Managed Emotions," so you can openly discuss their importance. Look under the "Emotions are Contagious" part of the Youth Journal Chapter One.

You can also demonstrate the ability yourself to say things like these statements in response to the young person's questions or upsetting situations:

> "No, that question is too personal. I'm not going to discuss that. I keep that private from everyone except two certain people. You'll have feelings and situations like that in your own life, and I respect your boundaries too."

Or:

> "I understand how frustrating and upsetting that situation is for you. I can help you use your skills in dealing with this or getting assistance from someone who can help. But I can't do anything about it for you myself."

Dealing with Difficulties

Difficulties could arise while you are working with your young person. Here are few and how you could deal with them:

Resistance: It is not unusual for learners to resist discussing certain topics, doing writing exercises, or doing any of this work. We recommend that you take a two-step approach:

1. **Empathize**: Let them know you empathize with their resistance. "I can understand not wanting to bother with this, or that it seems too hard (12-year-olds) or that it seems too easy (some 17-year-olds)."

2. **Educate**: Give them some information they may not have. "But many people have learned these skills and written these exercises and are glad they did. Now, they can use them anywhere in their lives. And they remember them better because they wrote them down."

Tears or Anger: It's possible that talking or writing about these skills may trigger some tears or anger for them. Let him or her know that it is okay to take a break for a few minutes while they calm themselves down. You can just sit with them. Don't try to talk them out of their tears or anger, or try to counsel them or ask probing questions. We don't want to open up emotions except with a professional counselor. Instead, just tell them to use their skills by giving themselves an encouraging statement. You can help them think of one.

Skill 1. Managing Your Emotions

Before you meet with your young person, read this chapter in the Youth Journal to get familiar with the ideas and exercises. Think of some examples that you could give to help him or her understand the concepts in the chapter. They can be personal, just not too personal as described above.

The main point of this chapter is to understand the positive role that emotions can play in our lives and relationships, as well as the negative role they can have in overwhelming us and preventing us from thinking clearly and problem solving.

Make sure to read the explanation in the Youth Journal of how the brain has two types of brain responses to problems: Logical Brain and Reaction Brain. While we have often referred to these as "Left Brain" and "Right Brain" responses, neuroscientists say that it isn't that clear cut, so we are moving to using Logical Brain and Reaction Brain, because each of these uses parts of both brain hemispheres. But for teaching purposes, left brain and right brain help remember the general idea. Everyone knows we're not brain scientists.

Also, read about the brain's response to stress by releasing cortisol and adrenaline. We want the youth to understand that these stress hormones can just take over on their own and drive reaction without thinking. However, a big part of adolescence is teaching our brain when these reactions are necessary and when they are not.

Encourage your teen to regularly ask himself or herself: "Is this really a crisis?" That question alone will help in managing their emotions. Stop and think! As soon as they slow down and start thinking about whether it is a crisis, they will have a better chance at getting their response to fit the situation.

Are emotions contagious? Yes. Understanding that and protecting others from emotions that are too intense for the situation is another important part of managing our emotions. We can inappropriately unload our emotions on others, and others can inappropriately unload theirs on us. This awareness will help your young person build emotional boundaries to protect himself or herself and others nearby.

Goal-setting is the last exercise in this chapter. Think back to our discussion of goals in Chapter One in this *Instructor's Guide*. Did you ask your teen about their goals for this course? If they told you some, now is a good time to remember and discuss them. Keep in mind that their goals do not have to be fancy or long or "SMART" goals, even though we mentioned that concept in the *Youth Journal*. But some older teens might want to set SMART goals, so help them decide if their goals are specific, measurable, attainable, relevant and time-focused.

Skill 2. Flexible Thinking

Again, read this chapter in the Youth Journal before you meet with your young person. Get familiar with the concepts. Think of some examples to help explain the difference between "all-or-nothing" thinking and "flexible" thinking. Think of some times one helped you or made a situation harder.

Generally, flexible thinking works better than all-or-nothing thinking. But, of course, your young person may think of a time when all-or-nothing thinking was a good idea. For example, if a friend wanted you to jump off a cliff into some water fifty feet below and you didn't know whether there were rocks under the water, that's a good situation in which to say, "Absolutely not!" Flexible thinking is flexible enough to allow a few occasions for all-or-nothing thinking, but they are few and far between.

Making Proposals: Decision making by making and responding to proposals (suggestions, ideas, options, solutions, etc.) is an important lesson in this chapter. This is a good place for practicing the three steps of Making Proposals by coming up with a scenario that can relate to your teen:

Step 1: One person makes a proposal (who does what, where & when)

Step 2: Other person(s) ask questions (first person answers them)

Step 3: Other person(s) say: "Yes," "No," or, "I'll think about it."

As explained in the *Youth Journal*:

> By asking questions, it keeps people from just rejecting the proposal, especially if they are upset with the proposal. Instead, it pushes everyone to use their Logical Brain by thinking of questions and answers.
>
> One of the best questions is to ask, "What would your proposal look like in action?" This way you can get clearer on the Who, What, Where and When of the proposal. You might even ask: "What's your picture of how this would work? What would you do? What would I do, if you could picture your proposal actually happening?"
>
> Then, the answer can be brief:
>
> "Yes," means you have an agreement, a plan. Just work out the details and do it. Yay!
>
> "No," simply means you need to make a new proposal or suggestion. Keep making proposals until you can both agree on something.
>
> "I'll think about it," is a good answer because that means it is being taken seriously, but the person needs more time or needs to get more information. In a tense situation, this often relieves the tension so that everyone can keep using their Logical Brain—which works a little slower than the Reactions Brain. Just agree on how much time the person needs to think about it.

Learning this skill can be very important when it comes to teenagers making decisions, including: having sex, running away, spreading rumors, stealing, publicly humiliating someone as a joke, etc. There are so many situations in which two or more young people make decisions, but they don't think about it as a conscious decision—they just do it! Learning about proposals will help them make better decisions.

Try to do a practice situation in which you each play someone making a proposal and then someone responding with questions. Answer with "Yes," "No," or "I'll think about it." You can make this fun. In fact, feel free to make all of this learning with crazy examples or take ones from a TV show, movie or the news.

Goal-setting is the last exercise in this chapter also. Help your young person remember his or her goals from the beginning conversation you had, if you talked about goals at the start of working together. Again, these can be simple or SMART goals, if you are working with an older teen.

Skill 3. Moderate Behavior

Again, read this chapter in the *Youth Journal* before you meet with your young person. With this chapter you can discuss a lot of behaviors that are extreme and a lot that are moderate. Unfortunately, there are a lot of extreme behaviors shown on television, movies and social media these days. You can ask your young person which behaviors they think are extreme and which are moderate. The Youth Journal asks them to give examples of each and this can lead to some good discussions.

At this point in the *Youth Journal*, we give an example of how these three skills are connected. How you think influences how you feel, which influences how you act or behave, like this:

Thoughts

↓

Feelings

↓

Actions

> It's almost like dominoes, one triggers the next, triggers the next. Of course, we usually aren't even aware that this is what is happening. It can be so fast and not even conscious.

You can explain that you can try to make any of these three go well and it will influence the others. Keeping your thoughts flexible will help you feel better rather than feeling trapped in a situation. Managing your emotions will help you control your own behavior so that you don't overreact and make things worse. And practicing a new, moderate behavior may actually change how you feel and how you think. "I didn't realize that I could succeed at that. Now I feel great! I think I will do that again sometime."

In this chapter, the youth will learn about using BIFF responses to hostile texts or emails containing misinformation. BIFF stands for Brief, Informative, Friendly and Firm. This is another important specific skill to help your teen practice more than once. You could pretend to write nasty comments to each other and then write BIFF responses to them. This skill can be very helpful in dealing with cyberbullying and teenagers are the most vulnerable to this.

Here is a short explanation of this skill from the Youth Journal:

The BIFF Response® Method

The BIFF Communication Method was developed to give a moderate response to hostile or misinformed emails and other writings. This is one of the biggest areas these days where extreme behavior comes out a lot. The BIFF method has four characteristics:

BRIEF: By only writing 2-4 sentences, you don't give the other person much to react to or criticize. A BIFF response can fit with any writing you receive of any length. Four pages of hate mail? Just respond with 2-4 sentences. Two sentences of accusations? Just 2-4 sentences for the response.

INFORMATIVE: Don't focus on how you feel. Don't defend your actions. Don't criticize what the other person said. Don't give your opinion. Don't give an emotional response. Just provide some factual, objective information on whatever the topic is. This puts your response into their Logical Brain, rather than triggering their Reaction Brain unnecessarily.

FRIENDLY: Just a friendly greeting or brief cheerful comment or closing in your BIFF can help the other person calm down. You don't have to be super friendly, but it helps to keep the tone somewhat friendly so you don't trigger their Reaction Brain unnecessarily.

FIRM: This doesn't mean harsh. It just means that you try to end the conversation rather than keeping it going back and forth with nasty comments. Sometimes you might need some information or a decision from the other person. In that case, try to put it into a question that they can answer with a Yes or No response. Also, ask for a response by a certain day and time, otherwise they may never respond.

Ideally, your young person can bring a sample hostile text and their proposed response to it. You can help them examine their response by asking these ten questions:

1. Is it Brief?

2. Is it Informative?

3. Is it Friendly?

4. Is it Firm?

5. Does it contain any advice? (That just escalates things.)

6. Does it contain any admonishments? (That's like talking down to them.)

7. Does it contain any apologies? (The reader might use it against you.)

8. How do you think the other person will respond?

9. Now, is there anything you would take out, add or change?

10. Would you like to hear my thoughts about it?

These questions are described in depth in our little book *BIFF: Quick Responses to High Conflict People, Their Personal Attacks, Hostile Email and Social Media Meltdowns.*

By asking these questions before giving your own thoughts (Question #10), you help the young person reflect on what they have written in a way that will help them in the future with things they will write as texts, emails or even formal letters.

The issue of avoiding apologies in BIFF responses is that many angry people see things in all-or-nothing terms, so that they will take the apology as your admission that it IS all your fault. We have seen this happen in too many cases. So, this is not the place for an apology. Of course, with most reasonable people, an apology in person can be very effective. But with potentially high conflict people, we try to leave those out of our BIFF responses.

Goal-setting is the last exercise is this skill chapter. Again, help them come up with any goal that works for them, whether simple or complex.

Skill 4. Checking Yourself

This is the fourth skill and the one that reminds them to keep on top of using the other skills. It also helps them remember not to become preoccupied with blaming others but instead focusing on their own behavior and what they could do differently. We teach that you can't control someone else's behavior, but you can control your own response to it.

This is your last chance to help the teen plan for the future, perhaps an upcoming difficult situation in the coming week or two. You can talk through how they could use all four skills in handling the situation. You could suggest that they take notes of what they decide they want to say in that difficult situation, such as an encouraging statement for himself or herself, how they will manage their emotions and what type of moderate behavior they intend to use.

Verification of Completion

After this fourth skill has been understood and practiced, you can sign the Certificate of Achievement in the back of this *Instructor's Guide* for your young person.

Congratulations

to both of you!

You and your young person have finished

New Ways for Life™!

CHAPTER THREE

Teaching *New Ways for Life*™ as a Class
By Susie Rayner

We developed *New Ways for Life*™ to be an engaging class for young people, whether you approach it individually or with a group of young people. To accomplish this, we developed optional additional materials which can be obtained from our website: www.NewWays4Life.com. They do not automatically come with this *Instructor's Guide*.

Additional materials include:

» PowerPoint slides

» Games

» Posters

» Feelings cards

You can use any of these along with the Instruction Pages in the following sections of this *Instructor's Guide*. Or you can use the Instruction Pages contained herein alone without the other materials and simply refer to the Feelings Words Guide at the end of this *Instructor's Guide*.

Each Teacher/Coach/Facilitator will have a specific way of teaching, however we ask that you align yourself with the "my level" or "same level" delivery method we mentioned in our Letter From Us to You at the beginning as we believe this method will encourage greater motivation for learning.

Young people are not programmed to be at their A-game all day. We recommend that you engage young people in the morning. After lunch, their brains are ready to hit the wall and may have a harder time absorbing the program or comprehending, or they just switch off!

Let your young people be the experts. Let them know that you recognize their expertise and you need their help if change is going to happen. Let them know that they are in charge of their learning, not you. You gather resources and tools for them, but it is up to them to use them.

For the first session, we recommend bringing something that is going to build rapport and trust with your young people. Sometimes it is easier for them to share their feelings with someone they know. By sharing something about yourself and your experiences, this helps to lower anxiety. Be sincere, use humor and smile. Share something that will let them know that you've been their age once, such as an old school report, a photo of when you were their age, a diary you have kept, or a story of your time in school.

The *Instructor's Guide* will help you to engage your young people more effectively. It will help you to understand what motivates them, and create an environment where they feel free to express what is important to them, what it's like being them and how stress affects them.

There is time for question and discussions. The *New Ways for Life*™ method is flexible but structured at the same time.

Sessions Overview

Session 1: Managing Emotions

Session 1 is about building rapport and really connecting with your young people. Think about why you wake up in the morning, and try to understand what motivates your young people. Create an environment where they feel comfortable raising their hand to ask questions. Listen and respect what they share, no matter how insignificant it may seem. Tell a story of your experience from their age. Bring a photo, story, or something that engages them. This session is about "Managing Emotions," our brains and stress.

Session 2: Flexible Thinking

Session 2 will introduce BIFF responses, teaching best practices for young people to utilize their brains and manage stress. You will facilitate conversations with your young people, discussing events from the previous Session and the application of what they have learned thus far. Youth will be introduced to how we can apply "Flexible Thinking," and avoid the trap of "all-or-nothing thinking."

Session 3: Moderate Behavior

Session 3 will also involve reflecting on events of the previous Session, and applying principles that have already been taught. This Session will introduce how we can use "Moderate Behavior" instead of extreme behavior, and will review BIFF responses.

Session 4: Checking Yourself

Session 4 is the final Session. You will, again, facilitate discussion reflecting on how the young people have implemented skills they have learned. You will introduce how to "Check Yourself" rather than blaming others for what is happening.

Key Aspects to Convey in the Class

> » Essential skills for everyday life
>
> » Easy to understand
>
> » Four sessions of 30-45 mins each
>
> » Non-traditional method of teaching, using discussions in which young people can communicate their feelings
>
> » We are all on the same level here. All young people are "A & B" students in your room until they prove you wrong!
>
> » Introduce the Youth Journal and explain that they will need to fill this out throughout the program and bring to each class. There is no required homework, but they can choose to read ahead.

Working with Additional Materials

If you decide to obtain the additional materials (www.NewWays4Life. com), you will receive four presentations, including PowerPoint slides. Each presentation has several slides to be discussed. You will deliver a different skill in sequence to teach your young people. There are corresponding Instruction Pages for each slide. Each page in the *Youth Journal* and *Instructor's Guide* are also identified. As you move through the program you will have the chance to reflect and re-cap what was learned the Session before, ensuring understanding and clarifying any misconceptions.

With each Session there is additional content which can be discussed that directly relates to each of the **4 Big Skills**.

Each PowerPoint slide has a corresponding Instruction Page for you. The instructions will ensure that you are discussing the correct content for each slide, and it will also give you the chance to emphasize and focus on putting yourself in their shoes. Focus on starting a conversation rather than teaching. If your young people are engaged in a conversation, then the understanding will flow from connection. This is your chance to really engage with your young people and be on their level to deliver the content. It's imperative that you take the time to ask questions and make sure that your young people have comprehension of the skills.

You will know your young people are on the right track by their conversations. Some may take longer to understand, but it is important to celebrate and emphasize the small successes when they occur. Small successes that are noticed are great reinforcers for understanding.

Each of your young people should obtain a Youth Journal which they can use with each of the sessions. There is no homework for this program, just life practice.

What can I get from the www.NewWays4Life.com website that can be used with this *Instructor's Guide* (all are optional but may be helpful)?

> » Session 1 Presentation (PowerPoint 20 Slides)
>
> » Session 2 Presentation (PowerPoint 12 Slides)
>
> » Session 3 Presentation (PowerPoint 16 Slides)
>
> » Session 4 Presentation (PowerPoint 10 Slides)
>
> » Access to resources on the *New Ways for Life™* website
>
> » 4 Games / Exercises—1 for each session
>
> » Poster for your classroom or space
>
> » Brief email support from *New Ways for Life™*, if required
>
> » Membership in the New Ways Pro Group

Class Session 1:
Managing Emotions
30 - 45 mins

Welcome:

Select a song that is upbeat and something that will connect with your young people. Play this song at the beginning and end of this session as your young people enter and leave the classroom or space.

Be energized and throw off good vibes! Let your youth know you are excited about this program. This way you will be able to truly welcome and connect with your young people.

Introduction: Brief story from the Teacher / Coach / Facilitator

Gather together your material or story that will help you to be on the same level with your group (a story that relates to when you were the age of the young people that you are teaching, a photo, a school report, etc.).

Engage with your young people. **Be mindful to be on the same level.** It may be a challenge for some facilitators to relinquish being in control and teaching, but it's fundamental to the success of *New Ways for Life™*.

Skill 1: Managing Emotions

Our Brains and Stress

Game: Feelings Cards (available at www.NewWays4Life.com). You can refer to the list of emotions on the Feelings Word Guide at the end of this *Instructor's Guide* to assist in this discussion. What are emotions? Discuss.

Q & A (**The conversations**): It's vital that the conversations are throughout each session. This will keep your young people communicating, and will also let them feel they have control of what they want to say.

The *Youth Journal:*

A learning tool for the young people to keep for future use

Designed to keep your youth on track throughout the sessions

The space for learning must be **caring, supportive, understanding and non-judgmental.** Everyone in the room is equal. They are all "A & B" Grade students until they prove to you that they are not. Whatever is happening in their private lives may be affecting their schooling, their friendships and their entire life. You want your young people to feel that by learning these skills they will be able to better process various situations in their lives.

Use the PowerPoint slides (available at www.NewWays4Life.com) and Instruction Pages in sequence to ensure maximum content delivery.

Inform each young person that there is no required homework or exams for this program.

The following instructions parallel the PowerPoint slides obtainable from www.NewWays4Life.com.

Slide 1A: Instructions

Tell your young person/people the following in your own words:

Our time together is about being in the moment, not thinking about what we are doing later or on the weekend. It is not much time to be in the moment. In this course you will learn life skills that you can use in almost any situation, good and bad. These skills are empowering, and you will see how easy it is to take control of your world.

Key aspects to convey:

Be welcoming!

Convey that these are life skills for almost any situation

Your youth can take control of their world by utilizing these principles

Slide 2A: Instructions

Tell your young person/people the following in your own words:

You may be struggling with some of your class work or your homework. You may have a problem, but you don't know how to bring it up with your parents. Or you might just be having a hard time. After this course, you will have new ways to deal with stressful and difficult situations.

You will be able to respond accordingly to other peoples' emotional roller coasters. You will be able to recognize a toxic situation and choose how to deal with it. Life does get stressful at times! Things happen that are out of your control, but the key is to be aware.

Our goal, together, is to talk about and understand the **4 Big Skills**: our emotions, our behavior, our thinking, and our response to stress. How do the **4 Big Skills** intertwine on a day to day basis? How do we use BIFF responses? This is a funny acronym we will discuss in the coming Sessions.

Key aspects to convey:

Awareness of personal struggles and stressful times

General introduction to the **4 Big Skills** and BIFF responses

Conversation to have:

"Put your hand up if you think you've got a few things that you're struggling with at the moment? Put your hand up if you think it would be great to sort them out?"

Reference in *Youth Journal:*

N/A

Slide 3A: Instructions

Tell your young person/people the following in your own words:

Here we have what we call **4 Big Skills**. The first is Managing Your Emotions. Managing Your Emotions will help you to reduce stress, and control how you react to it. By managing your emotions, you will feel better, act better and able to think of solutions to problems that come up in your everyday life. If you have unmanaged emotions, you can't make decisions or be rational about the decisions you make.

The second skill is called Flexible Thinking, having choices. Flexible Thinking will help you when you are looking for solutions. Another way to look at it is: you can choose to change your mind.

There is always more than one solution to any problem. If you don't use flexible thinking, you will be using what we call "all or nothing thinking." All or nothing thinking creates a barrier for problem solving. It keeps us stuck in old ways. You could look at it as being "one eyed," or "It's my way or the highway." Flexible Thinking allows us to explore other options, and choose the one that is best for our situation and for all people involved.

The third skill is using Moderate Behavior. We will go into detail about Moderate Behavior later on in the course, but the general concept is that we should try to avoid overreacting. Sometimes the way people react to a difficult or stressful situation is with extreme behavior. This often gets people into trouble, sometimes serious trouble, like going to jail. Extreme behavior is usually driven by extreme feelings.

The fourth skill is Checking Yourself. This skill forces you to reflect on the first three skills. Ask yourself, "Am I calming and managing my emotions? Am I using flexible thinking and am I using moderate behaviors?" Keep checking yourself. It's easy to forget when you're in an upsetting situation. Checking yourself may be the most important skill because, if you stop and check yourself, you're much more likely to have success.

Key aspects to convey:

The **4 Big Skills**

Conversation to have:

"Have you heard of these skills before? Now you know what the skills are, do you think that these skills will help with the problems that you're having?"

Reference in *Youth Journal*:

N/A

Slide 4A: Instructions

Tell your young person/people the following in your own words:

You guys are the lucky ones. I didn't learn these skills until now. If I had been taught these skills when I was younger, things would have been a lot different.

These skills will assist with the relationships that you're going to have in the future: friends, teachers, parents, family, and work colleagues.

You'll come up against difficult times in your life and school, which could include taking exams or breaking up with a boyfriend or girlfriend. Deciding on a future career and looking for a job after high school or college can also be stressful and challenging. It might seem like a sensory overload in the moment, and a sea of 'it's just too much' or overwhelming feelings. By learning and implementing these skills, life won't seem so out of control.

Key aspects to convey:

This is a golden opportunity to make real change in a short space of time, an opportunity that will be positive in your world now and in your future.

These are skills for everyday use. Once you know them, you can apply them to almost any situation.

We know you're going through a lot but you have this chance to really make a difference to yourself. These skills are for you.

When you know the skills and use them, contentment and calm will be all around you.

Conversation to have:

Talk to your group about the end of a relationship. How did they deal with it?

"By a show of hands, who would like to feel in control of their future? That's what we are here to do."

Reference in *Youth Journal:*

N/A

Slide 5A: Instructions (Title Slide)

Skill 1. Managing your Emotions. How to deal with how you are feeling

Slide 6A: Instructions

Skill 1. Managing your Emotions and Stress

Tell your young person/people the following in your own words:

Upset feelings are just feelings, and they can be managed.

We need to think specifically about which feelings to act on and which feelings to set aside. In other words, this means managing upsetting times. It makes sense, because being able to manage your own stress impacts you in two ways:

» Lowers your anxiety levels

» It's a realization that it is possible to manage stress

It also means you're "emotionally available." You're not always reacting defensively, but instead you are truly able to focus on yourself, what is happening, and why these feelings are happening. Most importantly, what should you do with them?

Key aspects to convey:

We can deal with how we are feeling.

Which feelings should we act on, and which should we set aside?

Conversation to have:

Talk about feelings. Use the Feelings Word Guide at the end of this *Instructor's Guide* to talk about some of the feelings that your group has experienced over the last few Sessions or months. **But be careful not to go too deep into feelings, or the young people may become overwhelmed.** Focus on identifying feelings, understanding feelings, thinking about feelings and learning skills for managing feelings.

Reference in *Youth Journal:*

N/A

Slide 7A: Instructions

Skill 1. Managing your Emotions and Stress

Tell your young person/people the following in your own words:

Emotions are normal. What do we do with them?

Feelings are information which can help us. Often times, we act before we think. For example, you could be feeling angry about what someone has said to you. In response, you yell, ignore them, send them a nasty text message, or tell them in an abusive, verbal way to go away. This is acting before thinking. If we just act without thinking, we can often make things much worse. Instead, we should take our feelings into account and consider including them in what we do. We all get angry, but how we deal with this feeling is key. If we can deal with how we are feeling, we can work out which feelings to act on and which feelings to set aside.

Key aspects to convey:

Emotions are normal.

Think about and understand what we are feeling.

Which feelings to act on and which to set aside

Reference in *Youth Journal:* Page __

Introduction of Youth Journal.

Read "What is stress?"

Discuss Writing Exercise #1: How have you handled your upset feelings?

Discuss Writing Exercise #2: How have you calmed yourself?

Slide 8A: Instructions

Tell your young person/people the following in your own words:

Calm Yourself!

By taking a break when you are angry, sad or frustrated, you give yourself time to calm down. Do something that you find relaxing. You could go for a walk., listen to music or maybe even take a nap.

You could also talk to someone neutral, someone who will listen and give you encouragement without lecturing or trying to solve your problems for you. A person who wants to get involved in the problem or who will also get upset isn't someone neutral and may make things worse. If possible, it is best to talk to a person outside the conflict. Choose someone to call or text and say, "I just need someone to listen for a few minutes. Can we chat?"

These emotions will not last forever. After 20-30 minutes, you should be calm, and able to think more clearly.

Being in control of your life and having realistic expectations about your day-to-day challenges are the keys to stress management, which is perhaps the most important ingredient to living a happy, healthy and rewarding life.

Is anger a feeling to act on or think about before we act?

Key aspects to convey:

Calming upset emotions

How can we calm ourselves?

Stress causes all sorts of health issues. It is important to manage your stress!

Conversation to have:

Stress can cause lots of illnesses. Can you think of any?

Reference in *Youth Journal*: Page ___

Read "Calming Yourself"

Discuss Writing Exercise #3: What can I do? Calming yourself.

Slide 9A: Instructions

Tell your young person/people the following in your own words:

Our brains work differently in times of stress. Most of the time we use our **Logical Brain** (generally Left Brain) for problem solving. However, in times of stress or crisis, we use our **Reaction Brain** (generally Right Brain) to respond to an event more quickly in case our survival is at risk.

Check time (you should have about 25 mins left of your session.)

Key aspects to convey:

Our brain is complex. To keep this basic, simply say that we have 2 sides of the brain (hemispheres), with a different emphasis for what each does, but there's lots of overlap.

We need to understand these two different approaches to problem-solving and stress.

Reference in *Youth Journal:* Page ___

Read "Stressful Times"

Discuss Writing Exercise #4: Which brain studies for a test?

Discuss Writing Exercise #5: Which brain avoids a speeding truck?

Discuss Writing Exercise #6: Our brains under stress

Slide 10A: Instructions

Tell your young person/people the following in your own words:

The Logical Left Brain pays a lot of attention to words, problem solving, planning and remembering how problems were solved in the past. When you are "thinking," most of the time you are probably thinking with your "left brain." This includes solving problems dealing with daily life (walking to school, talking to your friends, and learning at school.) Some researchers say the left brain is dominant most of the time.

Key aspects to convey:

The left brain is generally our logical, problem solving brain.

Conversations to have:

Have you heard of the left and right side of the brain? Obviously, it's much more complex than that. This is just a basic way to look at the brain and how it functions.

Reference in *Youth Journal*:

N/A

Slide 11A: Instructions

Tell your young person/people the following in your own words:

Our Right Brain thinks in many creative and intuitive ways and pays a lot of attention to what's going on around our environment. This includes people's emotions, their facial expressions and their voices. When you're in a crisis or a brand-new situation, the right brain becomes dominant, especially the defensive part of your right brain: The Reaction Brain. But it's much more than that.

Key aspects to convey:

Right brain is our Creative part of the brain but it's also responsible for your emotions and your defensive reactions.

Conversation to have:

What side of the brain do you think you use most of the time?

Are you constantly becoming defensive? Or reacting badly? Does it feel like a switch is being flicked inside you and you're suddenly angry or sad?

Reference in *Youth Journal*:

N/A

Slide 12A: Instructions

Tell your young person/people the following in your own words:

The defensive part of your right brain helps you protect yourself from danger. This seems to be the driving part of deciding whether you need to fight, flight or escape the situation, or freeze and hide as if you're not there.

The fight, flight or freeze response seems to be driven more by the right brain. It has a lot of other functions, but these defenses seem to primarily act in the right side of the brain.

When you're feeling really defensive in the right brain, you are energized and may feel intense negative emotions. Anger, fear, hate, dread, hurt – all of those kinds of negative emotions give you power and energy to save yourself in a life-and-death situation.

However, most of the time we are not in a life or death situation, so that kind of intense emotion can be inappropriate and actually get us into trouble.

How do the researchers know what the left and right sides of the brain control? They have studied brain MRIs to examine how the blood is flowing and the human response to various emotions. They can see a lot of blood flow activity in the right brain when someone is upset, and more blood flow activity in the left brain when someone is calmly solving a problem.

Key aspects to convey:

The right brain is where defensive reactions are primarily located.

We are not normally in fight, flight, or freeze circumstances in our everyday life.

The right brain is where our intense emotions come from. The left brain is where our calmer, problem solving ways come from.

Conversation to have:

Ask, "What happens in your house when you are angry?" Facilitate conversation about what happens and how they could be reacting defensively when they don't need too.

"Does your parent(s) get angry? Could they be reacting defensively without knowing it?"

Reference in *Youth Journal:*

N/A

Slide 13A: Instructions

Tell your young person/people the following in your own words:

The left brain seems to have more calmness, contentment and mild emotions associated with it. That makes sense if you're reading a book, having a friendly conversation with somebody, or solving a problem. When we're solving problems, like doing puzzles and games, we're likely to feel good.

A problem is created when you're really upset. You can't think straight, and intense emotions are causing this overwhelming feeling coming from the right brain.

You need to understand this: The right brain reactions shut off the left-brain problem solving.

Key aspects to convey:

Right brain sets off defensive reactions

Right brain shuts off the left brain (problem solving)

Understand that this happens when we are stressed or in a situation where we are angry, frustrated or really upset.

Conversation to have:

Ask, "Do you think that this has happened to you when you were angry or stressed?" (You couldn't think straight? Why do you think that happened?)

Reference in *Youth Journal:* Page ___

Discuss Writing Exercise #7: What did you learn?

Slide 14A: Instructions

Tell your young person/people the following in your own words:

How do we calm the defensive emotions enough so that we can start to think again and solve problems? We can use encouraging statements to calm ourselves. Encouraging statements help us to keep our composure and not react defensively.

Let's think of some encouraging statements we can use to help us keep our calm. When you're playing sport "You can do it!" might be effective. Make sure that your encouraging statements are not comparing yourself to someone else. "I'm better at this than them," is not what we want. "I am good at this," is a better option.

Having an encouraging statement will help you when you're in an upsetting situation. Remember how the brain works: Most of the time, the left brain is dominant. That's the more thinking, problem-solving brain. When you're feeling calm and comfortable, it's really easy to tell yourself, "I'm am pretty good at this." It is not so easy when your right brain is momentarily shutting this part down. When you're upset and you are in the defensive reactive thinking (that is part of the right brain,) it's so much harder. In fact, people's minds just go blank sometimes. It often helps to talk to your friends about how you're feeling and talk about your emotions. Girls may be better at doing this, but guys, you need to talk too! Two heads are better than one.

Key aspects to convey:

We are able to, and sometimes need to, calm ourselves down. It is important to ensure our defensive reactions don't take over, causing us to not be able to think straight.

It is useful to have a few encouraging statements for those times when you are going to be a bit stressed, angry or frustrated.

Conversation to have:

In whole or small groups ask, "Who has this happened to: You've been so angry that you haven't been able to think straight? How did you respond? Could you have responded more calmly or rationally?"

Reference in *Youth Journal:* Page ___

Read encouraging statements

Discuss Writing Exercise #8: Our brains under stress

Discuss Writing Exercise #9: Encouraging statements by others

Discuss Writing Exercise #10: Encouraging statements of your own

Discuss Writing Exercise #11: Planning ahead for encouraging statements under stress

Slide 15A: Instructions

Tell your young person/people the following in your own words:

Brain research has shown that emotions are actually contagious. He tend to mirror each other. If someone is feeling happy, others around him/her start to feel happier too. If someone is feeling sad, those nearby may also be feeling sad. Sometimes you will find that people, friends or family may pressure you into feeling the way they are.

Being aware of the idea that emotions are contagious can help us to stop and think about the emotional reaction we are having and why we may be reacting this way. Just because someone else is upset, it doesn't mean that you have to have the same feelings. You are responsible for your own feelings. Being aware allows us to have better control over how we respond to certain situations.

It is important not to get sucked into someone else's feelings. It won't serve you well. Throughout your life, you will see many different emotional situations arise. These may be at home, school or when you're playing sport. Some may be positive and some may be negative. I want to remind you that you don't have to have the same feelings and you are responsible for how you feel.

Key aspects to convey:

Emotions are contagious - you can catch them

Stop and think about how you are going to react. How do you feel about the situation?

Conversation to have:

Ask, "Has anyone pressured you into feeling the way that they were feeling, even though you were not feeling that way?"

Reference in *Youth Journal:* Page ____

Discuss Writing Exercise #12: Emotions are contagious

Discuss Writing Exercise #13: Picking up on others' emotions

Slide 16A: Instructions

Tell your young person/people the following in your own words:

It's all about being aware, being in the moment, and being responsible for your own feelings.

Just because someone else is perhaps having a disagreement and they are angry, sad or frustrated at another person doesn't mean that you need to take on those emotions. Don't get caught up in what they are feeling. It doesn't mean that you can't empathize with them. You can support them, but be aware of your own feelings about the issue.

Another really cool part of having contagious emotions is that it also has the reverse effect. We can calm other people's upset emotions. This is a BIG positive! If we can stay calm when others are upset, they will often calm down as well. Remember that our right brain shuts down our logical problem-solving brain.

It's really important to have **empathy**. Empathy is different from sympathy. Having empathy for someone means that you feel the pain, frustration, sadness or anger that another person may be feeling. Empathy may come from possibly having had the same feelings in your very own life. It lets the other person know that you are concerned about them and that you can relate to their upset emotions. An example of responding with empathy would be, "I can see how failing your driving test is really frustrating for you. I understand this is really important for you."

Sympathy is also really important. Having sympathy for someone is letting them know that you can see they are in a bad situation. You may feel sorry for them or be sad for them. Responding with sympathy may sound like, "That really stinks you didn't pass your driver's license test. What a bummer!"

Key aspects to convey:

Being responsible for your own feelings

Don't get caught up in what others are feeling

Emotions are contagious. You can calm other people's upset emotions by letting them catch your emotions.

Responding with Empathy and Sympathy

Conversation to have:

Empathy vs Sympathy: Ask your young people to think of a time they felt empathy or sympathy for someone. To make sure they understand the difference, have the young person or group identify whether it was an empathetic or sympathetic response.

Reference in *Youth Journal:*

N/A

Slide 17A: Instructions

Tell your young person/people the following in your own words:

As you can see from the picture, the issue starts out small but gets blown way out of proportion. It's like a volcano erupting and it doesn't stop. Here is an example of how picking up on others emotions makes things worse:

The anger could start from a text message. You get a nasty text, you respond with a nasty text, they respond with an even worse text that really hurts you. Then you respond with something really awful that hurts them back. Can you see how the escalation starts, and it doesn't stop until you become aware that emotions are contagious? When you stop and think and refuse to respond with anger, you can actually de-escalate an issue. If you are aware, you can calm yourself and then focus on problem solving.

One way to de-escalate this scenario is to not text back. But if you must, don't get involved with the back and forth banter. Just stop responding. Next Session we will talk about how to respond to texts.

Key aspects to convey:

» Stop the escalation. Calm yourself (perhaps with an encouraging statement), and be aware of your right and left brain.

» Focus on problem solving rather than reacting defensively.

Conversation to have:

Ask, "Have you ever had a back and forth conversation that got heated because you were not aware of emotions being contagious?"

Reference in *Youth Journal:*

N/A

Slide 18A: Instructions

Remind your young people that it's all about focusing on problem solving rather than getting into defensive reacting or thinking. They must remember that they can override their defensive thinking.

Key aspects to convey:

You can control your own thoughts and behaviors. Don't get into defensive reacting or thinking.

Conversation to have:

Any questions from your young people?

Reference in *Youth Journal*:

N/A

Slide 19A: Instructions

Tell your young person/people the following in your own words:

Even music can create an energized feeling or make you feel good. Sometimes having multiple feelings at one time can be a bit confusing or even overwhelming. It's likely that you will feel strong emotions when there are big changes in your life, like starting something new. You might feel a bit scared and excited at the same time. Working out what you're feeling will help you to calm yourself.

In this situation, it's a really good idea to talk about these feelings. Break them down into individual feelings: Happy, sad, excited, nervous, angry and/or frustrated. Talk about these feelings or write them down. Remember when we talk about things, it can calm us down. Using our left brain can help us manage our emotions.

Learning to control your behavior when everything around you is out of control is a valuable skill, and a character trait that a lot of people aspire to have. Practice, practice, practice! Keep practicing. You may slip up every now and again, but soon it will become normal behavior. You will be aware of your own emotions and how to react to others.

Key aspects to convey:

» You can control your own thoughts and behaviors

» Do not get into the cycle of reacting or thinking defensively

Conversation to have:

» Facilitate conversation about issues that your young people have.

» Ask, " Has anyone had a mixture of emotions? What did you do?"

Reference in _Youth Journal_:

N/A

Slide 20A: Instructions - Q & A Time

Session 2:
Flexible Thinking
30 - 40 mins

Welcome:

Select a different song from last Session that is upbeat and something that you like and they possibly won't. This plays into the skill of this Session, having "Flexible Thinking." Play this song at the beginning and end of the session as your young people enter and leave the classroom or space.

Be energized and throw off good vibes! Let your youth know you are excited about this program. This way you will be able to truly welcome and connect with your young people.

Introduction: Brief story from the Teacher / Coach / Facilitator

Gather together your material or story that will help you to be on the same level with your group (a story that relates to when you were the age of the young people that you are teaching, a photo, a school report, etc.).

Engage with your young people. **Be mindful to be on the same level.** It may be a challenge for some facilitators to relinquish being in control and teaching, but it's fundamental to the success of *New Ways for Life™*.

Skill 2: Flexible Thinking

Game – What's important to me?
(available at www.NewWays4Life.com)

Q & A (**The Conversations**): It's vital that the conversations are throughout each session. This will keep your young people communicating and will also let them feel they have control of what they want to say.

The Youth Journal:

A learning tool to keep for future use

Designed to keep your youth on track throughout the sessions

The space for learning must be **caring, supportive and understanding and non-judgmental.** Everyone in the room is equal. They are all "A & B" Grade students until they prove to you that they are not. Whatever is happening in their private lives may be affecting their schooling, their friendships and their entire life. You want your young people to feel that by learning these skills they will be able to better process various situations in their lives.

Use the slides (available at www.NewWays4Life.com) and Instruction Pages in sequence to ensure maximum content delivery.

Inform each young person that there is no required homework or exams for this program.

Slide 1B: Instructions (Title Slide: Flexible Thinking)

Slide 2B: Instructions

Briefly review the concept from Session 1: Managed Emotions.

Tell your young person/people the following in your own words:

This Session is about Flexible Thinking. There is always more than one way to solve a problem or more than one way to look at things.

Key aspects to convey:

We will be working on another skill to layer on top of the first skill we now know from last week.

Conversation to have:

Did anyone have a chance to use "Managing their emotions" over the past week? Would anyone like to share with the group what happened?

Reference in *Youth Journal*:

N/A

Slide 3B: Instructions

Tell your young person/people the following in your own words:

In our last session, we looked at how we can manage our emotions by using encouraging statements. We also learned that emotions are contagious and that we can control our own emotions. We now know a really important function of the brain: the right brain overrides and shuts down our left side when we are stressed out or in a dangerous situation. The Reaction Right Brain is valuable when we need to go into fight, flight or freeze mode, but we are not typically in this situation. We need to be aware that our defensive reactions are coming from our Reaction Right Brain and not our Logical Problem-Solving left brain.

Key aspects to convey:

> » Let's look at solving the problem rather than being one-eyed.
> » Another way to look at Flexible Thinking is having a choice.

Conversation to have:

Did anyone use an encouraging statement during the past week? What happened?

Reference in *Youth Journal:*

N/A

Slide 4B: Instructions

Say, "Today we will add Flexible Thinking to our skill set."

Slide 5B: Instructions

Tell your young person/people the following in your own words:

We can solve problems if we think flexibly.

1. Figure out the problem. This is where you need to manage your emotions so that you can think straight and let your left brain do its job: Problem Solving.

2. Once you have realized that this is not a life or death situation and you don't need to use your defensive reacting, you can then look at the options you have to solve your problem.

This could be a situation where you have done something you knew was wrong, you have made it worse, and now you don't know what to do. Even if you don't know what to do, that is ok! You are predominantly using your left brain to solve the problem, which is where you can think a little less defensively.

Key aspects to convey:

Problems can be solved if you Think Flexibly.

Conversation to have:

» Ask, "Who gets defensive when they have unmanaged emotions?"

» "Do you think things will be different now that you know you can manage your emotions and solve problems? If you flip out, do you think you will be aware and know why you are flipping out? If this happens, realize that your left brain has been hijacked!"

Reference in *Youth Journal:* Page ___

> » **Discuss Writing Exercise 14:** Goal for managing your emotions

> » Solve a problem using Flexible Thinking

Slide 6B: Instructions

Tell your young person/people the following in your own words:

What is Flexible Thinking? Flexible Thinking helps you get along with others by being open to solving problems in a way you may not have considered. Thinking this way will allow you the opportunity to try new things. It's how we shift from one way of doing something to another. Learning this skill is invaluable in social situations and in school settings.

It is hard when you try and explain how something could be done and the other person doesn't see it your way. You wish they would! In the same way, they may wish that you saw it from their point of view. Seeing both ways is good because, together, you can work out what might be the best solution to move forward. Some people are very skilled at flexible thinking, while others are not. Think about some people you know. Do they use Flexible Thinking?

Key aspects to convey:

> » We don't always see from the other person's perspective, but it helps if you can.

> » If we don't use flexible thinking it can often get us into a situation that we could have avoided.

Conversation to have:

» You are late to class and your teacher has asked that you stay back after the class to make up for the lateness. What would be a flexible thinking response to this?

Reference in *Youth Journal:* Page ___

» **Discuss Writing Exercise #15:** Using Flexible Thinking to Solve a Problem

» Practice Solving a Problem

Slide 7B: Instructions

Tell your young person/people the following in your own words:

The opposite of Flexible Thinking is all-or-nothing thinking. This type of thinking keeps us stuck. It is very one-eyed. No one likes a person with an "it's my way or the highway" attitude. People like this make you feel like your point is not valid or they don't care what you think. It is also a barrier to moving forward. There are options. You will always have choices and it's up to you to see them.

People often say that they would love to know what the future holds. Unfortunately, nobody knows what the future holds. If you could predict the future, then it would be ok to have "all-or-nothing" thinking. There would be no need for you to come up with alternatives to a problem because you already knew exactly what was going to happen.

Key aspects to convey:

> » Flexible thinking allows for change

> » Using this way of thinking gives you the chance to be able to explore new things.

Conversation to have:

> » Ask, "Can you think of a time that you had no flexibility in your thinking? What happened?"

Reference in *Youth Journal:* Page ____

> » **Discuss Writing Exercise #16:** Solving a problem

> » Other people and their way of thinking.

Slide 8B: Instructions

Tell your young person/people the following in your own words:

What is All-or-Nothing thinking? It's like using a set of scales with all the weight on one side and nothing on the other. There is no meeting in the middle or any compromise.

Let's talk through some examples of all-or-nothing thinking. We all do it from time to time.

Who can give us some examples related to friendships? Teachers? An employer you have had?

It's hard to connect with someone that uses this way of thinking. It's very one-sided.

If you routinely practice all-or-nothing thinking, you will have difficulty connecting with people. They will start to think that it's too hard to talk with you because you have the opinion that everything you think is right, and won't listen to anyone else.

Key aspects to convey:

» It's hard to be friends with someone who uses all-or-nothing thinking. It keeps you stuck and doesn't allow for change.

Conversation to have:

» Talk with your group and ask them if they relate to any of the points raised on the slide. Ask them if they can think of some other all-or-nothing thinking scenarios that they have either used or have seen.

Reference in *Youth Journal:*

N/A

Slide 9B: Instructions

Tell your young person/people the following in your own words:

The opposite of all-or-nothing thinking is Flexible Thinking. This list has a few examples that relate to the previous slide. Each point is a Flexible Thinking response to the all-or-nothing responses on the previous slide.

When you use Flexible Thinking, there is room for movement in your thinking. Flexible Thinking is not all doom and gloom. We've all heard the saying, "There is light at the end of the tunnel!" It's so true. Just because someone says you can't do that, doesn't mean you can't find an alternative way to do it.

Flexible thinking gives you options, creates a space to see what else might happen or what else is available to you, and gives you hope and positivity. When you put it in your mind that there is always a solution, you will be more approachable, more collaborative and more open to change.

Key aspects to convey:

» Flexible Thinking gives the opportunity to change.

» Allows you to see from different perspectives

Conversation to have:

» Do you think you are more of an 'all-or-nothing' thinker or a 'flexible' thinker?

» Ask someone to tell you what they think you are.

Reference in *Youth Journal*: Page ___

» Discuss **Writing Exercise #17**: Other people and their thinking

» Discuss **Writing Exercise #18**: Flexible Thinking solution

Slide 10B: Instructions

Tell your young person/people the following in your own words:

Let's connect with our brain. It's so unconscious that we are not even aware it's happening, just like breathing. At the moment we are using our left brain. We are talking, communicating and discussing. We are working on answers to questions and we are calm. Being aware is really crucial. When we are calm, we can work on dealing with stressful situations or anxious moments in better ways. The conversations we have with our parents might be difficult conversations. Maybe you don't want to talk to them or might not agree with what they are saying. This is all-or-nothing thinking. Your parents might want to talk to you about your phone use or the way that you speak to them. Using Flexible Thinking will help in these situations, opening you up to possibilities and better relationships. If we use flexible thinking, this helps to let you see that all is not lost. There is another way.

Key aspects to convey:

» It's ok to have different opinions. Allow yourself to listen to what others have to say. It may be a window of opportunity for you.

» Talk to yourself as if the world is your oyster. If something doesn't go your way, be flexible in your thinking and try something else. You never know what might happen.

Conversation to have:

» Ask, "Have you been in a situation where you have been asked to do something and you didn't want to do it? Or you have told yourself, "What's the point?" If so, you've used all-or-nothing thinking.

Reference in *Youth Journal:* Page ___

> » **Discuss Writing Exercise #19:** Ways of using flexible thinking

Slide 11B: Instructions

To check for understanding, ask, "What is the Flexible Thinking response?"

Answer: The third response is the Flexible Thinking response.

Key aspects to convey:

N/A

Conversation to have:

> » Which is the most common response you use? 1, 2 or 3

> » What are you going to do in the future (that uses the Flexible Thinking response) ?

Reference in *Youth Journal:* Page __

> » **Discuss Writing Exercise #20:** Proposals and questions

> » **Discuss Writing Exercise #21:** What is your Flexible Thinking goal?

Slide 12B: Instructions

End of Session 2. Next week is Moderate Behavior.

Key aspects to convey:

> » Thinking in a flexible way is better than being an all-or-nothing thinker. All-or-nothing thinking keeps you stuck and shut off to possibilities in your future.

Conversation to have:

> » Do you have any questions about Flexible Thinking or anything else we covered last week?

Reference in *Youth Journal:*

N/A

Session 3:
Moderate Behavior and BIFF Responses
30 - 45 mins

Welcome:

Select a different song from last week, one that is upbeat and will help you connect with your young people. Play this song at the beginning and end of the session as your young people enter and leave the classroom or space.

Be energized and throw off good vibes! Let your youth know you are excited about this program. This way you will be able to truly welcome and connect with your young people.

Introduction: Brief story from the Teacher / Coach / Facilitator

Gather together your material or story that will help you to be on the same level with your group (a story that relates to when you were the age of the young people that you are teaching, a photo, a school report, etc.).

Engage with your young people. **Be mindful to be on the same level.** It may be a challenge for some facilitators to relinquish being in control and teaching, but it's fundamental to the success of *New Ways for Life™*.

Skill 3: Moderate Behavior & BIFF Responses

Game: BINGO – Moderate & Extreme Behavior
(available at www.NewWays4Life.com.)

Q & A (**The Conversations**): It's vital that the conversations are throughout each session. This will keep your young people communicating, and will also let them feel they have control of what they want to say.

The Youth Journal:

A learning tool to keep for future use

Designed to keep your youth on track throughout the sessions

The space for learning must be **caring, supportive and understanding and non-judgmental.** Everyone in the room is equal. They are all "A & B" Grade students until they prove to you that they are not. Whatever is happening in their private lives may be affecting their schooling, their friendships and their entire life. You want your young people to feel that by learning these skills they will be able to better process various situations in their lives.

Use the slides (available at www.NewWays4Life.com) and Instruction Pages in sequence to ensure maximum content delivery.

Inform each young person that there is no homework or exams for this program

Slide 1C: Instructions (Title slide: Life Skills Program)

Slide 2C: Instructions

Ask, "What we have covered in the past 2 weeks?" (Answer: Manage Emotions and Flexible Thinking.)

Say, "We have 2 more sessions. We are halfway there!"

Key aspects to convey:

N/A

Conversation to have:

N/A

Reference in *Youth Journal*:

N/A

Slide 3C: Instructions

Re-cap Managing Emotions & Flexible Thinking

Key aspects to convey:

Say, "Like any new skill that we learn, it takes practice to master. There is no formal homework for this program, but I hope that you are all using your new skills and that they are helping you in everyday life."

Conversation to have:

Ask, "Did anyone have a chance to use Flexible Thinking since the last session? Did you need to Manage your Emotions? Did you find it difficult? What happened?"

Reference in *Youth Journal:*

N/A

Slide 4C: Instructions

Tell your young person/people the following in your own words:

This Session we are talking about behavior. How do we respond to situations when we are angry, frustrated, anxious, sad or happy? How do we respond to hurtful or nasty texts or messages on social media?

We will use Managing our Emotions, Flexible Thinking, and Moderating our Behavior and our responses to avoid over-reacting to situations that can be managed.

How do we act that is acceptable? How do we react that is acceptable?

Key aspects to convey:

N/A

Conversation to have:

N/A

Reference in *Youth Journal:*

N/A

Slide 5C: Instructions

Tell your young person/people the following in your own words:

In this course we look at 2 ways to react when we are in stressful or frustrating situations. We are specifically talking about your behavior. There are two ways you can behave: Moderately or Extremely. We will go into detail as we move through the content.

Key aspects to convey:

How do we react to stressful situations or those that make us feel sad, anxious, frustrated? What are the consequences if we react badly? Our behavior directly relates to what happens to us in life.

Conversation to have:

N/A

Reference in *Youth Journal:*

N/A

Slide 6C: Instructions

Tell your young person/people the following in your own words:

Extreme behavior is what we want to avoid. It is usually what gets us in trouble, and there are usually negative consequences. Extreme behavior gets us into situations that we shouldn't be in.

Some people have difficulty controlling emotions in stressful situations. We have already learned about Managing Emotions and that emotions are contagious. We've also learned that if we use Flexible Thinking it will help us solve problems rather than create new ones.

Extreme behavior will get you into trouble with the Law, your family, your teacher, your boss or even yourself.

Why does this happen? Extreme behavior is driven by extreme emotions. It's not ok. Just because someone is reacting or acting in an unacceptable way does not mean that it's ok for you to do it too.

Key aspects to convey:

Extreme behavior is brought on by extreme emotions.

Conversation to have:

Have you acted in an unacceptable way before? What did you do? Can you now see that it was extreme behavior and not acceptable?

Reference in *Youth Journal:*

N/A

Slide 7C: Instructions

Tell your young person/people the following in your own words:

The word "extreme" makes us think of very serious behavior, such as physically assaulting someone bad enough that they end up in the hospital. However, extreme behavior can be more mild, such as yelling at or hitting someone. It can be verbal or physical. It is also what you might do to yourself, not just to someone else, like self-harm or an eating disorder.

Key aspects to convey:

Extreme behavior is behavior we want to avoid using.

Conversation to have:

Can you add to the list? What do you think might be other forms of extreme behaviors?

Reference in *Youth Journal:* Page ___

Discuss Writing Exercise #22: Did I overreact?

Discuss Writing Exercise #23: How did I overreact?

Slide 8C: Instructions

Tell your young person/people the following in your own words:

Why does this happen?

Extreme behavior is bad behavior. Your emotions are running wild. Your right brain is having a party that turns bad. You could be angry at your parents or frustrated with your teacher. You could feel anxious. You could feel stressed or angry, and act out by punching something or someone. Your right brain is taking over. You have unmanaged emotions and you haven't used an encouraging statement. You're in an all-or-nothing mode of thinking. Your left brain has left the building. Remember this is your calm, problem solving brain. With extreme behavior, your left brain has been shut off.

Key aspects to convey:

Acting on feelings and not being aware of what's actually happening inside yourself is what leads to extreme behavior.

Conversation to have:

Can you think of a time that you over-reacted and used extreme behavior? What happened?

Reference in *Youth Journal:* Page ___

Discuss Writing Exercise #24: Moderate and Extreme Behaviors

Slide 9C: Instructions

Tell your young person/people the following in your own words:

Negative consequences are things that happen to you after you have used extreme behavior. These could include getting a detention, your parents limiting your phone usage, or losing the privilege of attending your favorite concert. There will always be negative consequences for extreme or bad behavior.

What we need to do is stop and think: Are my actions acceptable or unacceptable? Am I reacting in an acceptable manner or in an unacceptable manner? Once the extreme behavior has been done, it can lead you down a negative pathway, like a snowball effect. One extreme behavior leads to another.

Here is an example:

> Your parents take your phone away for two weeks. Can you think of a reason why they might do this? Obviously, this is something that you don't want to happen. You're angry, so you verbally attack them by saying, "It's so unfair! I wish I didn't live here!" You go to your room and you slam the door, another extreme behavior. Your parents get angry at you for your response and add another week to your previous consequence. Now you are more frustrated and kick the door, accidentally kicking a hole in it! Now your parents say that you can't see any friends for a month, in addition to going three weeks with no phone.

Can you see how the extreme behavior just keeps escalating if you keep using extreme behavior and unmanaged emotions?

What if you had used Managed Emotions and Flexible Thinking and were able to talk to your parents about losing your phone? Maybe you could have negotiated less time without your phone. Look what escalated instead!

Key aspects to convey:

There are consequences to extreme behavior.

Conversation to have:

What do you think might be some of the consequences if you were in a fight? Stole something? Verbally abused someone at school?

Reference in *Youth Journal:* Page ___

Discuss Writing Exercise #25: What did you learn about Moderate and Extreme Behaviors?

Discuss Writing Exercise #26: My Moderate and Extreme Behaviors

Slide 10C: Instructions

Tell your young person/people the following in your own words:

BIFF is a way to respond to a text on social media that may be nasty or hurtful. Responding with BIFF uses the skills that we have learned: Managing your Emotions, Flexible Thinking and Moderating Behavior. Sending nasty or hurtful text is responding with extreme behavior.

BIFF is a calm way of responding. Your response doesn't use unmanaged emotions, it doesn't use all-or-nothing thinking, and it is moderate rather than extreme.

73

B is for BRIEF

I is for INFORMATIVE

F is for FRIENDLY

F is for FIRM

Key aspects to convey:

BIFF is a calm way of responding to a hurtful or nasty text

Conversation to have:

Have you ever had a hurtful or nasty text or social media post?

Reference in *Youth Journal*: Page ___

Discuss Writing Exercise #27: Responding to nasty or hurtful texts

Discuss Writing Exercise #28: Responding to nasty emails

Slide 11C: Instructions

Tell your young person/people the following in your own words:

B is for BRIEF

Brief means you respond with one or two sentences. Being brief stops the negative back and forth exchange between you and the other individual.

Here is an example:

> You receive a nasty text. You respond with another nasty or hurtful text. They respond with something worse. Pretty soon, the problem has escalated. The more responses that go back and forth, the more you leave yourself open to being criticized. Sometimes what is said in the back and forth messages are so fueled with unmanaged emotions that they are actually not true. You begin using extreme behavior and there will be negative consequences. A rumor might be spread about you because of the other person's unmanaged emotions, which we now know causes extreme behavior. Being brief in your response will hopefully shut down the war that might start.

Key aspects to convey:

Being brief shuts down the back and forth. If you respond with nasty messages, it means that you are doing what you don't like being done to you.

Conversation to have:

Do you think you could be brief if you received a nasty text?

Reference in *Youth Journal*:

N/A

Slide 12C: Instructions

Tell your young person/people the following in your own words:

I is for INFORMATIVE

Avoid over-reacting with opinions, emotions or putting the other person down. No matter how much you want too. Two wrongs don't make right. In this situation, having unmanaged emotions, all-or-nothing thinking, extreme behavior and engaging in an unacceptable manner will make you appear just as bad as the other person. Engaging in a back and forth text war and an explosion of unwanted verbal attacks or accusations creates stress and anxiety. Add "nasty texts" to your extreme behavior list.

Key aspects to convey:

Don't add unwanted opinions, emotions or put the other person down.

Conversation to have:

Ask, "How do you think your responses stack up? Are you reacting with opinions, emotions and putting the other person down?"

Reference in *Youth Journal:*

N/A

Slide 13C: Instructions

Tell your young person/people the following in your own words:

F is for FRIENDLY

This doesn't mean you have to be friends or act as if you are. This means that you need to be friendly in your response. Responding in a friendly way keeps the other person from having a reason to get defensive. Remember that you want to avoid your own defensive reacting, too, if they respond in a way that is unkind. It won't get you very far. Remember to calm your upset emotions with an encouraging statement and don't verbally attack the other person. Manage your Emotions and use Moderate Behavior.

Key aspects to convey:

If you have nothing nice to say, don't say anything at all.

Conversation to have:

Ask, "Do you think that you could make some changes in the way you respond from now on?"

Reference in *Youth Journal:*

N/A

Slide 14C: Instructions

Tell your young person/people the following in your own words:

F is for FIRM

This is your opportunity to stop your stress and stop your anxiety. It will not serve you to keep going with the messages.

Being firm means that you can prevent the back and forth and the escalation of texts. It does not mean being hurtful. You can be firm by saying something like, "I am not responding anymore. Goodbye." This lets the person know that you are not going to get into the banter, it's firm enough without being offensive or hurtful, and it's friendly with the "goodbye" at the end.

Key aspects to convey:

Being firm doesn't mean being nasty or hurtful. It puts an end to the back and forth.

Conversation to have:

Ask, "Have you ever ended a text on a firm note? What happened? or What did you say?"

Reference in *Youth Journal:*

N/A

Slide 15C: Instructions

Ten things to keep in mind as you write a BIFF response:

1. Is it BRIEF?

2. Is it INFORMATIVE?

3. Is it FRIENDLY?

4. Is it FIRM?

5. Does it contain advice?

6. Are you being nasty?

7. Does it contain apologies?

8. How do you think the other person will respond?

9. Is there anything you would take out, add or change?

10. Should I get a friend to read it first?

Tell your young person/people the following in your own words:

BIFF responses may take time to learn but it's always nicer to send a BIFF response rather than a message that is going to create anxiety, stress, magnify the situation, invite defensive reactions, unmanaged emotions, extreme behavior and all-or-nothing thinking.

Key aspects to convey:

Make sure you have a friend read your message if you're unsure if it is a BIFF response. Use the ten points to refer to when you are responding to a nasty or hurtful text.

Conversation to have:

N/A

Reference in *Youth Journal:* Page ____

Discuss Writing Exercise #29: Practice responding with BIFF texts

Discuss Writing Exercise #30: Practice your BIFF text response

Discuss Writing Exercise #31: Review your recent texts

Discuss Writing Exercise #32: Using BIFF responses

Slide 16C: Instructions

Tell your young person/people the following in your own words:

So far we have discussed Managing Emotions (Session 1), Flexible thinking (Session 2), and Moderate Behavior and BIFF responses (Session 3)

Take a moment to think back to the start of the first Session. You've learned some amazing skills!

Key aspects to convey:

Review the three skills (Managing Emotions, Flexible Thinking, and Moderate Behavior)

Conversation to have:

Have your youth explain their understanding of the three skills and how they might use them at school or at home.

Reference in *Youth Journal:* Page ___

Discuss Writing Exercise #33: What was the most helpful part of this section on Moderate Behavior?

Discuss Writing Exercise #34: How can you use what you've learned about Moderate Behavior in your life?

Discuss Writing Exercise #35: Moderate Behavior Goal

Session 4:
Checking Yourself
30 - 40 mins

Welcome:

Select a different song from last Session, one that is upbeat and will help you connect with your young people. Play this song at the beginning and end of the session as your young people enter and leave the classroom or space.

Be energized and throw off good vibes! Let your youth know you are excited about this program. This way you will be able to truly welcome and connect with your young people.

Introduction: Brief story from the Teacher / Coach / Facilitator

Gather together your material or story that will help you to be on the same level with your group (a story that relates to when you were the age of the young people that you are teaching, a photo, a school report, etc.).

Engage with your young people. **Be mindful to be on the same level.** It may be a challenge for some facilitators to relinquish being in control and teaching, but it's fundamental to the success of *New Ways for Life™*.

Skill 4: Checking Yourself

Game: Fill in the Blanks
(available at www.NewWays4Life.com)

Q & A (**The Conversations**): It's vital that the conversations are throughout each session. This will keep your young people communicating, and will also let them feel they have control of what they want to say.

The Youth Journal:

A learning tool to keep for future use

Designed to keep your youth on track throughout the sessions

The space for learning must be **caring, supportive and understanding and non-judgmental.** Everyone in the room is equal. They are all "A & B" Grade students until they prove to you that they are not. Whatever is happening in their private lives may be affecting their schooling, their friendships and their entire life. You want your young people to feel that by learning these skills they will be able to better process various situations in their lives.

Use the slides (available at www.NewWays4Life.com) and Instruction Pages in sequence to ensure maximum content delivery.

Inform each young person that there is no required homework or exams for this program.

Slide 1D: Instructions (Title Slide: *New Ways for Life*™)

Slide 2D: Instructions

What has been covered so far: Managed Emotions, Flexible Thinking, Moderate Behavior.

Key aspects to convey:

N/A

Conversation to have:

N/A

Reference in *Youth Journal:*

N/A

Slide 3D: Instructions

This covers the last three sessions in slightly more detail. It is a summary of the content from the first three sessions. Read off the slide and/or ask your group questions about their retention of each skill.

Key aspects to convey:

These three skills go hand in hand and work together to help with stressful situations or times of anxiety or frustration.

Conversation to have:

Ask, "What is one key piece of information that you have remembered about these skills?"

Reference in Youth Journal:

N/A

Slide 4D: Instructions

Tell your young person/people the following in your own words:

> Sometimes we blame others for what is happening to us when really, it's up to us to sort out what is going on inside and out. It's pretty simple: You can be a victim of your circumstances or a survivor. Guess what? The outcome is totally in your hands! This is a hard concept to grasp, but by checking yourself, you can be the best possible version of you!

Key aspects to convey:

Checking ourselves is the last skill to learn.

Conversation to have:

What do you think "Checking yourself" means?

Reference in *Youth Journal:*

N/A

Slide 5D: Instructions

Tell your young person/people the following in your own words:

You may be feeling anger, frustration or intense stress. Remember to Check Yourself first before blaming others. This is about dealing with what's going on inside and outside of ourselves. Realizing that we have a very BIG part to play in what is going on, so much more than we think.

Checking Yourself is about pulling all the skills together. This is the most important skill. It reminds you to take check on your emotions, your thinking, and your behavior. Handle yourself with integrity, being honest and true to yourself and to others around you. Act in a way that if you were looking at the situation from the outside, you would be proud of your conduct. How you feel, think and act is your responsibility, not anyone else's. Own your responsibility and Check Yourself. Take a look in the mirror first!

Key aspects to convey:

It's the vital skill that pulls everything together and lets you stop and check in, like a little private meeting with yourself. A heart to heart. A pep talk from your coach - YOU!

Conversation to have:

Ask, "Do you just blame others first? Have you done that in the past and then realized that you played a part in what happened?"

Reference in *Youth Journal*:

N/A

Slide 6D: Instructions

Tell your young person/people the following in your own words:

Am I checking myself? In other words, am I living my best authentic life? Probably no, so we need to change that. Take a mirror and take a look at yourself. Yep, it's confronting, but you will know if you're not stacking up. Are you being difficult on purpose, testing the boundaries? Why? If so, this is not ok: it's definitely not acting with integrity. Only you can change how you react when a situation comes up that you don't like.

If you keep getting detentions, who is at fault? If your parents are constantly asking you to do your homework, it's for a good reason. Don't blame them for being worried about you or being on your back. They care!

Perhaps you are upset that your sister borrowed your favorite skirt without asking you first. Ask yourself, "Do I need to use an encouraging statement?" Maybe telling yourself, "It's ok. I don't need it today," will actually calm you down. Look at the reality: it's just a skirt. Do you really need to be that angry about it? Probably not! Check in with yourself!

Maybe you are really upset that your boyfriend dumped you via a text. Don't lose your mind, become a bundle of tears or send nasty texts. Think about the emotion. Sure, you'll be sad, maybe even angry, but we know that they are just feelings and they can be managed.

Another way to look at the intense emotions you are feeling about your boyfriend dumping you is that maybe he is just not the right person for you. If you are not with him, you'll leave yourself open to others that might be a better fit for you. That's Flexible Thinking.

Same story if you had a girlfriend end the relationship. It will leave you open to others who might be a better fit. There's a lot of people out there you will meet.

Are you using Moderate Behavior? It's not ok to bully or talk about someone in a bad way. Reacting with aggression, verbally attacking someone and being out of control is not ok. When we don't get our own way or we are really stressed, it's not ok to fly off the handle. We need to check our behavior. Is it contributing to making the situation worse and are you possibly going to get more stressed out?

Key aspects to convey:

Checking yourself first before blaming others

Use these four skills when you are in a stressful, anxious or frustrating situation

Conversation to have:

Ask, "What do you think Checking Yourself means? Do you think it is important? Why or why not?

Reference in *Youth Journal:* Page ___

Discuss Writing Exercise #36: How do I check myself?

Slide 7D: Instructions

Tell your young person/people the following in your own words:

Checking yourself will help to slow you down. This will help you to stay proactive rather than reacting in a way that might get you in trouble, might hurt someone's feelings or cause you to later regret what you've said or done.

Remember, it only takes 20-30 mins to calm yourself down. Your Reaction Right Brain takes over when you are in a stressful situation. You want to remain calm and problem solve instead. You are, most of the time, not going to be in a life or death situation.

Don't create a problem that was not there in the first place. You'll certainly create a problem if you are not using the four skills that you have been taught.

Key aspects to convey:

Recognize that you need to check yourself and understand that it slows you down.

Conversation to have:

Ask, "Can you see how, if you Check Yourself, it can make a huge difference to the outcome? Is it worth NOT checking yourself?"

Reference in *Youth Journal:* Page __

Discuss Writing Exercise #37: Checking your behavior using these skills

Slide 8D: Instructions

Stay in control, don't lose control!

Key aspects to convey:

Re-cap the **4 Big Skills**

Conversation to have:

Free conversation

Reference in *Youth Journal:*

N/A

Slide 9D: Instructions

Think before you act.

Key aspects to convey:

Think about using the four skills when you are faced with stress, anger, sadness or other intense emotions.

Conversation to have:

Facilitate conversation about some of the key points that they have taken away from the last four weeks. Do they think they are really important to use in their day to day lives?

Reference in *Youth Journal:* Page ___

Discuss Writing Exercise #38: Checking Yourself for Not Blaming Others

Congratulations!

YOU HAVE FINISHED THE CLASS!

CONGRATULATE YOUR STUDENTS/YOUNG PEOPLE

See certificate at end of this book.

Feelings Word Guide

Sad	Happy	Hurt	Cherished
Lonely	Hopeful	Ignored	Appreciated
Despair	Overjoyed	Judged	Understood
Disappointed	Calm	Rejected	Empowered
Bitter	Optimistic	Offended	Accepted
Sorrowful	Enthusiastic	Destroyed	Healed
Upset	Thrilled	Hated	Loved
Angry	Loving	Despised	Reassured
Disgust	Kind	Crushed	Saved
Hateful	Amused	Mistreated	Commended
Depressed	Supported	Forgotten	Esteemed
Weak	Strong	Bored	Determined
Hopeless	Comforted	Drained	Refreshed
Scared	Relaxed	Fatigued	Alert
Anxious	Encouraged	Powerless	Invigorated
Pressured	Assured	Exhausted	Creative
Nervous	Prepared	Sick	Healthy
Worried	Forgiven	Paralyzed	Inspired
Embarrassed	Beautiful	Indifferent	Motivated
Stressed	Certainty	Weary	Rejuvenated
Worthless	Brave	Stale	Focused
Guilty	Valued	Dejected	Renewed

CERTIFICATE

of Achievement

You've got this

NEW WAYS FOR LIFE™

Managing Emotions, Flexible Thinking, Moderate
Behavior, BIFF Responses Checking Yourself

Certificate Number   Date Completed

---   ---

Signature

About Us

Susie Rayner is a mediator, co-parenting coach and founder of Mediate Negotiate, a family dispute resolution practice in Australia. Prior to becoming a dedicated family dispute resolution practitioner and family coach in 2018, she held positions in the corporate arena for 20 years. She also works in other areas of dispute resolution and volunteers with organizations that support people in crisis, particularly the fires of 2019-2020 in Australia. She is co-author of New Ways for Life™ Teacher Guide and Student Journal with HCI co-founder, Bill Eddy.

Bill Eddy is a family lawyer, therapist, mediator and the co-founder of the High Conflict Institute based in San Diego, California, USA. For several years he was a Kindergarten teacher, then he became a youth counsellor and drug counsellor at a psychiatric hospital and outpatient clinic for 12 years. For the past 20 years, he has been a family lawyer and family mediator focusing on helping children, youth and parents going through separation and divorce by teaching skills and resolving conflicts along the way. He developed the *New Ways for Families* method in 2009, which has been used in family counseling and some family court systems in the United States, Canada and Australia. In 2010, he started developing the *New Ways for Mediation* method primarily for mediating high conflict disputes. In 2014, he co-developed the *New Ways for Work Coaching Method* for potentially high conflict employees and managers. He views the various *New Ways* methods as the answer to the problems of dealing with the increasing presence of high conflict personalities and situations in today's world.

CPSIA information can be obtained
at www.ICGtesting.com
Printed in the USA
JSHW020418310720
6941JS00001B/1